CORNERSTONES OF FREEDOM™

D0974828

THE GREAT DEPRESSION

BY MELISSA MCDANIEL

CHILDREN'S PRESS®

An Imprint of Scholastic Inc.
New York Toronto London Auckland Sydney
Mexico City   New Delhi   Hong Kong
Danbury, Connecticut

BRINGING HISTORY to LIFE

Content Consultant
James Marten, PhD
Professor and Chair, History Department
Marquette University
Milwaukee, Wisconsin

Library of Congress Cataloging-in-Publication Data

McDaniel, Melissa, 1964–
  The Great Depression/by Melissa McDaniel.
      p. cm.—(Cornerstones of freedom)
  Includes bibliographical references and index.
  ISBN-13: 978-0-531-23056-5 (lib. bdg.)
  ISBN-13: 978-0-531-28156-7 (pbk.)
  1. United States—History—1933–1945—Juvenile literature. 2. United
States—History—1919–1933—Juvenile literature. 3. Depressions—1929—
United States—Juvenile literature. 4. New Deal, 1933–1939—Juvenile
literature. I. Title.
  E806.M426 2012
  973.916—dc23   2012004792

Photographs © 2013: age fotostock/Everett Collection, Inc.: 18, 23; AP
Images: 49 (Reed Saxon), 55 (Stanley Troutman), 17, 31, 32, 39, 40, 44, 50,
57; Art Resource/Berenice Abbott/The New York Public Library: 48; Corbis
Images/Bettmann: 4 top, 19, 30, 45; Courtesy of FDR Library: 24, 28, 42,
43, 47; Getty Images: 26 (American Stock), 34 (Chicago History Museum),
cover (Fotosearch), 4 bottom, 20 (General Photographic Agency), 7 (NY
Daily News), 14, 58 (OFF/AFP); Library of Congress: 54 (Alfred T. Palmer),
37 (Arthur Rothstein), 51 (Clifford Kennedy Berryman), back cover, 36
(Dorothea Lange), 5 bottom, 46, 56 bottom (Elias Goldensky), 15 (Irving
Underhill), 33 (John Vachon), 11, 27, 35, 56 top; NOAA/National Weather
Service Collection: 38; Superstock, Inc.: 8, 10, 12 (ClassicStock.com), 2, 3, 22,
59 (Everett Collection), 5 top, 16 (Underwood Photo Archives); The Granger
Collection: 6; The Image Works/Photo12: 13.

Maps by XNR Productions, Inc.

Did you know that studying history can be fun?

BRING HISTORY TO LIFE by becoming a history investigator. Examine the evidence (primary and secondary source materials); cross-examine the people and witnesses. Take a look at what was happening at the time—but be careful! What happened years ago might suddenly become incredibly interesting and change the way you think!

Contents

I KNOW 3 TRADES
I SPEAK 3 LANGUAGES
FOUGHT FOR 3 YEARS
HAVE 3 CHILDREN
AND NO WORK FOR
3 MONTHS
BUT I ONLY WANT
ONE JOB

The Roaring Twenties

> "All the News That's Fit to Print."
>
> ## The New York Times.
>
> THE WEATHER
>
> VOL. LXVIII...NO. 22,206.
>
> NEW YORK, MONDAY, NOVEMBER 11, 1918. TWENTY-FOUR PAGES.
>
> TWO CENTS
>
> ### ARMISTICE SIGNED, END OF THE WAR!
> ### BERLIN SEIZED BY REVOLUTIONISTS;
> ### NEW CHANCELLOR BEGS FOR ORDER;
> ### OUSTED KAISER FLEES TO HOLLAND
>
> SON FLEES WITH EX-KAISER
>
> Hindenburg Also Believed to be Among Those in His Party.
>
> ALL ARE HEAVILY ARMED
>
> Automobiles Bristle with Rifles as Fugitives Arrive at Dutch Frontier.
>
> ON THEIR WAY TO OG STEEG
>
> Belgians Yell to Them, "Are You On Your Way to Paris?"
>
> Kaiser Fought Hindenburg's Call for Abdication; Failed to Get Army's Support in Keeping Throne
>
> By GEORGE RENWICK
>
> BERLIN TROOPS JOIN REVOLT
>
> Reds Shell Building in Which Officers Vainly Resist.
>
> THRONGS DEMAND REPUBLIC
>
> Revolutionary Flag on Royal Palace—Crown Prince's Palace Also Seized.
>
> GENERAL STRIKE IS BEGUN
>
> Burgomaster and Police Submit—War Office Now Under Socialist Control.
>
> Socialist Chancellor Appeals to All Germans To Help Him Save Fatherland from Anarchy
>
> WAR ENDS AT 6 O'CLOCK THIS MORNING
>
> The State Department in Washington Made the Announcement at 2:45 o'Clock.
>
> ARMISTICE WAS SIGNED IN FRANCE AT MIDNIGHT
>
> Terms Include Withdrawal from Alsace-Lorraine, Disarming and Demobilization of Army and Navy, and Occupation of Strategic, Naval and Military Points.
>
> By The Associated Press.

The end of World War I came as a great relief to people all around the world.

America crackled with energy in the 1920s. World War I had ended in 1918. The soldiers were home, the **economy** was booming, and people were ready to have a good time. It was the go-go twenties. Night after night, middle-class Americans filled movie theaters and crowded into dim, hot nightclubs to work up a sweat dancing the Charleston and the Lindy Hop.

In homes across the country, jazz music blared out of brand-new radios. All sorts of new products were streaming off assembly lines: telephones, refrigerators, phonographs, fans, electric heaters, vacuum cleaners. Some of these devices had been around for years, but now even middle-class people could afford them. At the same time, America entered the age of the automobile. In 1915, there were about two million cars in the United States. By 1929, the nation was producing more than four million cars per year. Automobiles were no longer just for the rich.

Many middle-class people were also investing in the **stock** market. Stock values soared higher and higher. It seemed like the party would never end. But in late 1929, the economic bubble finally burst. The Great **Depression** had begun.

The Charleston was a popular dance throughout the 1920s.

THE CITY OF CHARLESTON, SC.

CHAPTER 1

THE CRASH OF 1929

More Americans bought cars during the 1920s than ever before.

THE PROSPERITY OF THE 1920S

was built on a shaky foundation, but it gave the American people almost limitless optimism. The rich got richer, and the middle class grew to include a major part of the country's population. Americans were bursting with confidence about their lives, the economy, and the country's future.

Refrigerators and other helpful appliances became common items in American middle-class homes during the 1920s.

More and More

Americans were told that they could continue to improve the country by spending more and more money. Some **economists** even claimed that saving money was foolish. Spending money would help eliminate poverty, said some government officials. In response, people bought cars and homes and household goods.

Many people did not have enough savings to buy these goods outright. Instead, they borrowed money to buy the products they wanted. Many stores set up a new process called **installment** buying. Buyers paid a little bit of money when purchasing a product. The rest was paid in installments over the course of months or years. This system worked well for everyone, at first. People did not have to wait until they had saved enough money to buy the items they wanted. Factories hummed night and day to keep up with the demand for these goods. Business was booming.

A Rising Market

People also spent money on stock. Stock sales provide companies with the money needed to expand their businesses. In return, the stocks serve as investments for the people who buy them by increasing in value as

U.S. factories produced a wide variety of goods, including radios, during the economic boom.

a company becomes more successful. The Dow Jones Industrial Average is a measure of the value of the stock of 30 large companies. It is an important sign of the U.S. economy's strength. In 1929, it was four times as high as it had been just five years earlier.

Many Americans, including some economists, believed the stock market had become a sure bet. Almost everyone saw it as an easy way to get wealthy. Some thought it was such a great investment that they borrowed money from their **stockbrokers** to buy the stock. This is called buying on margin. Some people paid as little as 10 percent of the stock's actual price. They borrowed the rest of the money.

Stockbrokers are experts in the stock market.

Investors struggled to unload all of their stocks as prices began to fall.

As the value of stocks shot up, more people invested in the market. This pushed prices up even more. Such **speculation** caused stocks to become worth far more than the companies they represented.

Going Down

In September 1929, stock prices began to fall. As they fell, many investors got nervous. They wanted to sell their stocks before prices dropped even more. This caused stock values to enter a downward cycle. With more people trying to sell stocks and fewer people wanting to buy, prices continued to plummet. Those who had borrowed

Plummeting stock prices caused a frenzy on the trading floor.

money to purchase their stocks were in trouble. They had no way to pay back what they owed, and the stocks themselves had little value. Many people went **bankrupt**.

Then, on Thursday, October 24, the market's decline went from a gradual slide to a sudden plunge. People were shocked, and panic took hold. Investors wanted to sell their stocks before they became totally worthless. Thirteen million shares of stock were sold that day—more than on any other day in history.

Over the weekend, President Herbert Hoover spoke about the troubled stock market. His words were broadcast over the radio into living rooms across the country. "The fundamental business of the country . . . ," he said, "is on a sound and prosperous basis."

But he was wrong. Stock prices fell even farther on Monday. By the end of the day, the Dow Jones Industrial Average had dropped 22.6 percent.

Black Tuesday

When the bell rang to signal the opening of trading at the New York Stock Exchange the following day, the cries of "Sell!

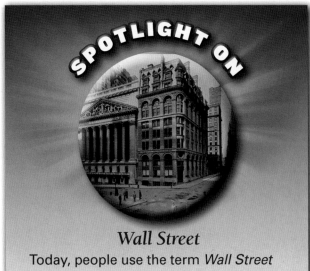

Wall Street

Today, people use the term *Wall Street* to refer to all of the nation's banking and financial industries at once. But Wall Street is also an actual street in Lower Manhattan. At one time, there was even a wall on Wall Street. It was built in 1653 to protect the tiny community of settlers there from being attacked by outsiders.

These days, Wall Street runs for just a few blocks. The New York Stock Exchange has been located on or near Wall Street since 1792. Over the years, many other stock exchanges and banks have also been located in the area. Wall Street remains the heart of the city's financial district.

Sell!" were incredibly loud. Everyone wanted out of the market. A guard at the stock exchange described the shock felt by the stockbrokers. He recalled, "They roared like a lot of lions and tigers. They hollered and screamed, they clawed at one another's collars. It was like a bunch of crazy men. Every once in a while, when [a big company] would take another tumble, you'd see some poor devil collapse and fall to the floor."

As the stocks lost value, many wealthy people lost their fortunes. Many middle-class people lost their life savings—and hope. People flooded onto New York City's Wall Street, the center of finance in the United States, hoping to find out what had happened to their money. But there was nothing anyone could do. The money was gone.

By the end of the day, more than 16 million stocks had been sold, a record that would stand for 40 years. The Dow Jones Industrial Average had dropped another 12 percent that day. Thousands of investors lost

The stock market crash made headlines across the nation.

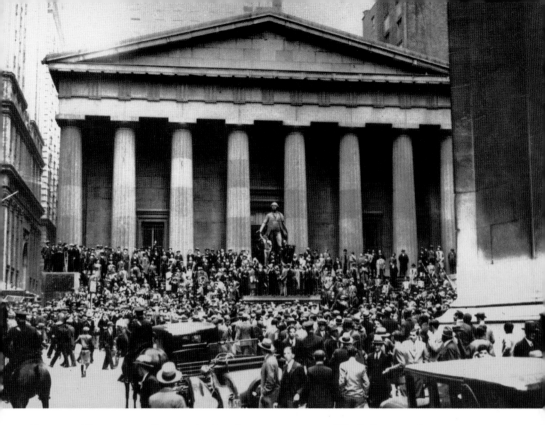

Extra police were dispatched to keep peace on Wall Street after the stock market crash.

everything. To this day, October 29, 1929, is known as Black Tuesday. It was the beginning of the Great Depression.

A FIRSTHAND LOOK AT
TICKER TAPE

In the 1920s, stock prices were printed out on long rolls of narrow paper called ticker tape. Investors looked at the tape to see how stock prices changed for different companies over the course of the day. During the stock market crash of 1929, so many stocks were sold that the ticker tape machines could not keep up. See page 60 for a link to view ticker tape from Black Tuesday, October 29, 1929.

YESTERDAY'S HEADLINES

On October 30, 1929, headlines around the world trumpeted the news of the stock market crash. "Wall Street Lays an Egg," blared *Variety*, a paper covering the entertainment industry. The *New York Times* was more serious. "Stocks Collapse in 16,410,030-Share Day," said the top headline. The paper still held out hope. The headline continued, "But Rally at Close Cheers Brokers; Bankers Optimistic." The nation's crisis was only starting. Newspaper reporters had no way of knowing the trouble ahead.

Declining Business

The stock market crash caused major problems for the nation's banks. They had loaned huge amounts of money to investors and stockbrokers buying on margin. In 1929, two out of every five dollars loaned by banks went to buy stocks. Once the market crashed, no one could pay back these loans. Banks had very little cash on hand. Customers feared that the banks would run out of money and that the money in their savings accounts would disappear.

People flooded into the banks to withdraw their savings. Because of this, many banks did run out of cash and were forced to shut down.

Many people lost all of their money in the crash. Those who did have money were afraid to spend it. People only bought things that were absolutely necessary. Factories could no longer sell all the goods they were making. They were forced to cut back on production. This meant that they needed fewer workers, so they laid employees off. Such job loss left even fewer people with money to buy anything. As a result, businesses suffered and laid off even more workers. All across the country, people were left penniless. It was the beginning of a dark, difficult decade.

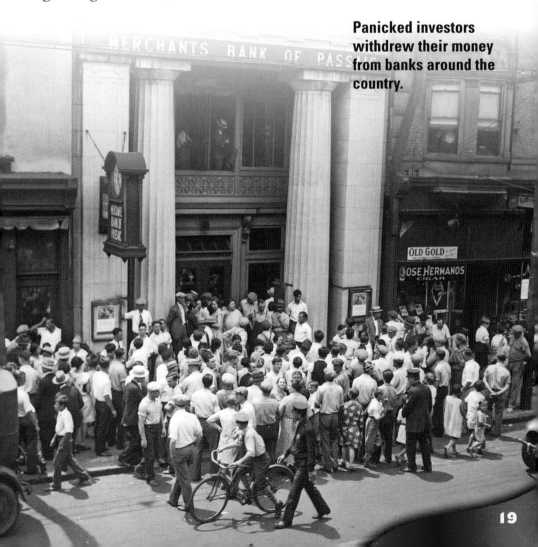

Panicked investors withdrew their money from banks around the country.

CHAPTER 2

STRUGGLING TO GET BY

The Depression took a heavy toll, financially and emotionally, on millions of people around the world.

I KNOW 3 TRADES
I SPEAK 3 LANGUAGES
FOUGHT FOR 3 YEARS
HAVE 3 CHILDREN
AND NO WORK FOR
3 MONTHS
BUT I ONLY WANT
ONE JOB

TODAY, PEOPLE WHO LOSE
their jobs often receive unemployment benefits
to help them get by as they look for work. But
unemployment programs did not exist at the start
of the Great Depression. Neither did the Social
Security program that provides payments to the
elderly. Bank accounts were not protected from
bank failure the way they are today. There were no
government programs to feed people or keep them
in their homes. Private charities tried to help, but
the number of people in need was overwhelming.

Many men who had held good jobs during the boom of the 1920s were left unemployed during the Depression.

Hard Times

Life changed quickly after the stock market crash. Earlier in 1929, just 3 percent of people who wanted to work were unemployed. By 1933, the unemployment rate had jumped to 25 percent. That means a full one-quarter of the labor force—15 million people—was unable to find work.

More companies laid off workers or shut down entirely, and those that continued to operate tightened their belts. Many companies cut wages, some by as much as half. As a result, even people who still had jobs had trouble surviving. The millions who had lost their jobs were even more desperate. They had no income whatsoever.

Many families had no money to buy food, make rent, or pay for electricity. In cities, families crowded together in small apartments to save money on rent. Some families lit their homes with kerosene lamps to avoid using electricity. Meat became a luxury that most people could not afford. People grew vegetables in spare patches of land in order to feed their families.

SPOTLIGHT ON

Apple Sellers

During the Great Depression, people were desperate for any work they could find. Early in the Depression, apple growers were producing far more apples than they needed. The apples would rot if they weren't sold, so the International Apple Shippers Association sold them on **credit** to people without jobs. The jobless people set up stands on street corners and sold the apples for a nickel each. The apples were a cheap source of food and a way for the sellers to make money during tough times. In the fall of 1930, there were 6,000 apple sellers on the streets of New York.

Soup Kitchens

For many people, these money-saving measures were not enough. Americans were starving. Children scoured garbage cans and dumps for any scraps of food they could find. Men sat on streets, begging for handouts.

A FIRSTHAND LOOK AT

"BROTHER, CAN YOU SPARE A DIME?"

Songs about the struggle to survive poured from the radio during the Great Depression. One of the best-known songs of the era is "Brother, Can You Spare a Dime?" by Yip Harburg and Jay Gorney. The lyrics are from the point of view of a man who helped build America and now cannot find work:

Once I built a railroad, I made it run, made it race against time.
Once I built a railroad; now it's done. Brother, can you spare a dime?
Once I built a tower, up to the sun, brick, and rivet, and lime;
Once I built a tower, now it's done. Brother, can you spare a dime?

See page 60 for a link to hear the popular singer Bing Crosby perform this song.

Many people relied on soup kitchens for hot meals. Churches, political organizations, and charities made large vats of food and distributed it for free to those in

Soup kitchens were the only sources of hot meals for many unemployed people.

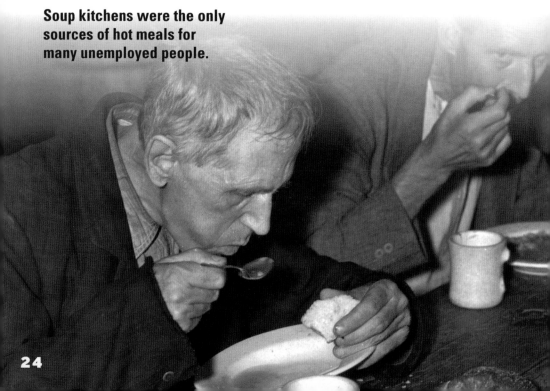

need. The food was simple, perhaps a thin soup and slice of bread, or a stew. But at least it was a little nourishment.

Soup kitchens sprang up in cities across the country. People sometimes arrived at the kitchens before dawn and waited in line for hours. They wanted to make sure they got a bite to eat before the food ran out. In 1931, in New York City, 82 soup kitchens were serving 85,000 free meals each day.

Lots of people felt that waiting in line and asking for handouts was humiliating. They were used to taking care of themselves and didn't like having to ask for help. But they had no choice.

A VIEW FROM ABROAD

The Great Depression was a worldwide crisis. It began in the United States but soon rippled around the world. Some nations were hit hard because they were heavily dependent on international trade. The economy of Chile, for example, was based on the **export** of copper and other products. U.S. businesses stopped buying these products as the Depression took a toll on their profits, and unemployment in Chile soared.

The United States had been giving aid to Germany to help it rebuild after World War I. Once the Depression started, the United States could no longer afford to help. The German economy, already suffering from the effects of the war, continued to fail. By 1932, the unemployment rate in Germany had reached 40 percent. This and other economic problems pushed Germany toward the extremism that led to World War II.

Hooverville shacks were constructed from any scraps of material people could find.

People outside of cities sometimes had more options. They could plant vegetables, collect wild berries and other foods, or hunt animals such as squirrels or rabbits. But it often wasn't enough. One sickly rural girl was told by a teacher to go home from school and get something to eat. "I can't," she replied. "It's my sister's turn to eat."

Hoovervilles

Poverty forced many people from their homes during the Great Depression. Without jobs or savings, they couldn't afford to make rent or **mortgage** payments. Those without family members to take them in were left homeless.

With nowhere to live, people built shacks and huts out of whatever materials they could find. They used cardboard and packing crates, tin cans and spare scraps of lumber. Communities of shacks sprang up all across the United States. They were called Hoovervilles. They were named after Herbert Hoover, who was president of the United States when the Great Depression began. People blamed him for not doing enough to help.

Many Hoovervilles were built along rivers, under bridges, or in parks. In New York City, there were Hoovervilles in Central Park and in Riverside Park along the Hudson River. One of the largest Hoovervilles in the country was in Seattle, Washington. It was home to about 1,200 people.

CHAPTER 3

FROM BAD TO WORSE

Schools were left with few resources during the Depressio[n]

cat
little cat
see a little cat.

AS THE 1930S WORE ON, the economy went from bad to worse. Because fewer people were working, fewer people were paying taxes. As a result, federal, state, and local governments had much less money. Many towns could not even afford to keep schools open. In 1933, 175,000 children missed out on their education because schools had closed for the year. In other places, the school year was much shorter than usual. For many families, the basic structure of life had broken down.

People who were willing to hop a freight train illegally were able to ride free to a new location.

Riding the Rails

Many people did not know where to turn. They looked around their towns and saw no chance of finding work. The only hope they had was in the unknown. As a result, people began to travel. They clung to the possibility that perhaps things were a little bit better in the next city or state.

Jobless people had no money to keep a car running or pay for a bus ticket. Some walked or hitchhiked, and many hopped on freight trains. "It was no trick for a swift, skinny kid to grab the rung of a ladder on a slow-moving freight, then climb up on top or swing into an empty boxcar, going who knows where," recalled John Gojack, one of the Depression's many unemployed travelers. But in fact, jumping on a boxcar was quite dangerous. Tens of thousands of people were injured or killed jumping on or off trains during the Great Depression.

When people jumped on trains, they did not know where they would end up. They jumped off wherever they could and began looking for work. Sometimes they found work picking fruits or vegetables for a short time. When the job was over, they hopped back on trains and headed to new towns.

Some people rode on unsafe parts of trains to avoid getting caught by railroad workers.

More than two million people rode the rails during the Great Depression. Most were men, but thousands of women did, too. Some of the drifters, who were often called hobos, later made names for themselves. H. L. Hunt, who became a billionaire in the oil industry, spent time as a hobo. So did Woody Guthrie, one of the most famous folksingers of the 20th century.

Woody Guthrie wrote such famous folk songs as "This Land Is Your Land" and "Pastures of Plenty."

Some of the hobos who rode the rails were very young.

Young People Adrift

It is estimated that a quarter million children and teenagers were traveling and living on the roads across the country during the Depression. Some left home to look for work. Others simply didn't want to be a burden to their families anymore.

Hobos often helped each other find food and shelter.

Many young people riding the rails traveled in groups, for safety. They were constantly on the move, and some found that they enjoyed the hobo lifestyle. They liked the challenge of looking for a place to sleep, a bite to eat, or a day's work. For some, it seemed like a grand adventure. "I loved it," a young drifter named Walter Ballard later recalled. "It'll get in your blood.

You're not agoing any-where, you don't care, you just ride. . . . You're going to eat, that was more than you was do-ing at home, probably."

The Dust Bowl

People living on the Great Plains had a second dose of trouble during the 1930s. **Drought** struck this vast stretch of flat land beginning in 1931. The rains did not return for most of the decade.

The Great Plains are made up of farm and ranch lands. The region is always dry, and trees are few and far between. The drought shriveled the crops and ground-covering plants that normally grew there. When winds whipped across the

YESTERDAY'S HEADLINES

One of the worst dust storms of the 1930s blew across the plains on April 14, 1935, a day that became known as Black Sunday. The storm made headlines in newspapers across the region. A story in the *Liberal News* of Liberal, Kansas, reported:

"A great black bank rolled in out of the northeast, and in a twinkling when it struck Liberal, plunged everything into inky blackness, worse than that on any midnight, when there is at least some starlight and outlines of objects can be seen. When the storm struck it was impossible to see one's hand before his face even two inches away."

plains, there were no plants to hold the dry topsoil in place. The wind picked up the dirt and carried it across the land in massive clouds. The Great Plains became known as the Dust Bowl.

In 1934, one huge dust cloud from the plains traveled all the way across the country. The dust made its way through New York City and continued out across

Drought left countless farms incapable of growing crops.

So much dust accumulated during storms that farmers had to raise their fences to keep them from being buried.

the Atlantic Ocean. Sailors on a ship 300 miles (483 kilometers) out to sea wrote their names in the dust that settled on their ships.

Back home on the plains, the dust blew into huge piles against the sides of houses. It covered tractors and clogged engines. It even seeped into houses through the tiniest cracks. One North Dakota woman recalled that after a four-day dust storm, dirt "lay inches deep on everything. Every towel and curtain was just black. There wasn't a clean dish or cooking utensil."

Dust storms ruined homes, destroyed equipment, and killed farm animals.

A FIRSTHAND LOOK AT
DOROTHEA LANGE'S PHOTOS

In 1936, a photographer named Dorothea Lange traveled around California taking photographs of **migrant** laborers. Lange's best-known photo is titled *Migrant Mother*. See page 60 for a link to view *Migrant Mother* and other photos by Dorothea Lange.

Heading West

People's livelihoods blew away with the soil. The drought continued, making the land impossible to farm. Many people believed there was nothing left for them at home and set off in search of better lives. By 1940, 2.5 million people had left the plains.

Some headed for the railroad tracks to join other homeless people in riding the rails. Many families headed for California. There, some became migrant farmworkers.

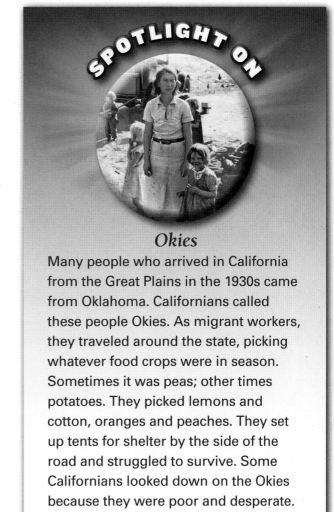

SPOTLIGHT ON

Okies

Many people who arrived in California from the Great Plains in the 1930s came from Oklahoma. Californians called these people Okies. As migrant workers, they traveled around the state, picking whatever food crops were in season. Sometimes it was peas; other times potatoes. They picked lemons and cotton, oranges and peaches. They set up tents for shelter by the side of the road and struggled to survive. Some Californians looked down on the Okies because they were poor and desperate. Okies were not made to feel welcome in California, but most stayed anyway.

The influx of people from the Great Plains overwhelmed Californians. In 1936, the Los Angeles police sent officers to the border to turn away newcomers who didn't have any money. Courts soon declared this illegal, saying that Americans had the right to travel wherever they wanted within their own country.

CHAPTER 4

THE NEW DEAL

Franklin D. Roosevelt delivered a passionate speech at the 1932 Democratic National Convention.

ON JULY 2, 1932, FRANKLIN Delano Roosevelt stood before a microphone at the Democratic National Convention in Chicago, Illinois. Roosevelt was the governor of New York, and he was about to become the Democratic candidate for president. He spoke confidently, and his words rang out through the convention hall and poured from radios in living rooms all across America. "I pledge you," Roosevelt's voice boomed, "I pledge myself, to a new deal for the American people."

Franklin Roosevelt was inaugurated as president on March 4, 1933.

Trusting Banks

Under President Hoover, the government had done little to help people without jobs or money. Hoover had urged businesses to stop laying off workers and called on charities to help the poor. Roosevelt offered a different approach. Under his New Deal, the government would establish new programs to help people directly. This promise helped Roosevelt win the presidential election in November 1932.

A FIRSTHAND LOOK AT
FIRESIDE CHATS

On March 12, 1933, just eight days after becoming president of the United States, Franklin Roosevelt gave his first fireside chat. He used the chat to try to calm people's fears. He also outlined his plan to make the U.S. banking system more secure. See page 60 for a link to hear a recording of the famous radio broadcast.

Roosevelt's first days as president saw a whirlwind of activity. A few days after taking office, he spoke over the radio in the first of his famous "fireside chats." From his office, Roosevelt spoke calmly to the American people, discussing his plans for the government and his optimism about the future.

President Roosevelt's fireside chats gave the American people hope that the Depression would soon be over.

Roosevelt ordered a bank holiday, temporarily shutting down banks to keep the Depression from getting worse. He then asked the Treasury Department to study each bank to determine whether it was financially stable. The government would help reorganize the banks that were in the worst shape.

Some New Deal programs were established to heal the economy and protect against future financial failures. The Federal Deposit Insurance Corporation (FDIC) was created to ensure that bank failures would no longer be able to destroy people's personal savings. The FDIC insured bank **deposits** up to $5,000. This meant that if a

President Roosevelt signed the Banking Act of 1933, establishing the FDIC and enacting stricter government controls over the way banks operate in the United States.

Joseph P. Kennedy (center) was the first chairman of the Securities and Exchange Commission.

bank went out of business, the government would make sure that account holders still got up to $5,000 back. Today, the FDIC insures much higher sums of money. The creation of the FDIC calmed many Americans. They could continue using banks without fear of losing their hard-earned money. Banks soon began to grow stable again as people started making more deposits.

The following year, Congress established the Securities and Exchange Commission (SEC) to supervise activities on Wall Street. The SEC is charged

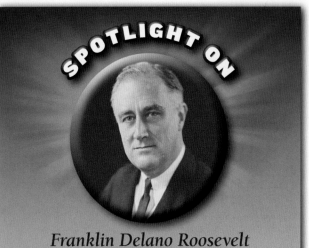

Franklin Delano Roosevelt

President Franklin Delano Roosevelt is best remembered for his efforts to help those suffering during the Great Depression. Born into a wealthy family, he himself never had to worry about money. But he faced other kinds of hardships. In 1921, he was struck with polio, a disease that often leaves patients unable to use their legs. For the rest of his life, he used a wheelchair. But he did not want people to know that he was disabled. In public, he wore metal braces on his legs that allowed him to stand.

As president during the Great Depression, Roosevelt offered many programs to help the country recover. He also provided the nation with energy and optimism. Roosevelt later led the country through most of World War II. He died in office a few months before the war's end. Franklin Roosevelt is the only president ever elected to four terms. After his time in office, the law was changed so that presidents could serve only two terms.

with ensuring that stockbrokers are fair in the deals they make. The government wanted Americans to be able to have confidence in the stock market once again.

Back to Work

Other New Deal programs were designed to provide unemployed Americans with jobs. As an added bonus, the new jobs would help improve the country in a variety of ways. The **Civilian** Conservation Corps (CCC) put young men to work in forests and parks. They planted trees and built trails and roads. The men were paid only a dollar a day, but they were given food and housing in the parklands where they

Members of the New Deal's CCC worked on a variety of projects to improve the country's outdoor areas.

worked. Many CCC workers saved their wages and sent the money back to their families. By 1936, one and a half million young men were working for the CCC.

A program called the Public Works Administration (PWA) was created to oversee large, government-funded construction projects. These projects included important structures such as bridges, tunnels, and dams. They put many people back to work. PWA projects included the

The WPA funded the work of photographer Berenice Abbott (see one of her photos above) and many other artists.

Lincoln Tunnel in New York City and the Grand Coulee Dam in Washington State.

The Works Progress Administration (WPA) also provided jobs to the unemployed. It built LaGuardia Airport in New York City and many scenic roads, among other things. It also created jobs for artists. Painters were hired to create murals in city halls. Photographers were hired to document life during the Depression. Berenice Abbott took to the streets of New York City, capturing the energy of the city with her striking photos.

The WPA sent writers around the country to write guidebooks for each state. Other writers interviewed elderly people who had lived under slavery. More than 2,300 former slaves told their stories. These interviews bring to life the experience of the brutal slavery system.

Safety Net

One of the New Deal's most enduring programs was Social Security, which was enacted by Congress in 1935. This program provides payments to the elderly, the unemployed, the disabled, and others. Roosevelt wanted to provide a safety net for all Americans and

TODAY'S PERSPECTIVE

One of the worst economic downturns to hit the United States since the Great Depression began in 2007. Before this crisis, many people were investing in real estate. Housing prices rose rapidly. Eventually, the prices collapsed. People were left with mortgage loans that were higher than the value of their houses. Many people went bankrupt.

The banking industry was also shaken. Large banks and other financial companies took part in risky loans and investments. Many were on the verge of collapse until the government stepped in to save them. Certain rules governing banks that had been enacted during the Great Depression had been relaxed in the years before 2007. Some experts believe that this contributed to the economic crisis.

Beginning with Ida May Fuller (above), Social Security benefits have helped countless people over the years.

reduce the suffering of those facing hardship. "I see no reason why every child, from the day he is born, shouldn't be a member of the social security system," he said. "When he begins to grow up, he should know he will have old-age benefits. . . . If he is out of work, he gets a benefit. If he is sick or crippled, he gets a benefit."

The first monthly Social Security check, for $22.54, was paid to Ida May Fuller of Vermont in 1940. Today, millions of people receive Social Security checks. In 2010, the program made payments of $712.5 billion.

Many other programs were also started under the New Deal. Some worked, others didn't. Critics thought that Roosevelt was spending too much money and expanding the government more than he should. But Roosevelt believed large problems required a large response. In his words, he was willing to "take a method and try it. If it fails, admit it frankly and try another. But above all, try something."

Many people criticized the New Deal as irresponsible government spending.

THIS IS ONE RABBIT THAT NEVER FAILED ME!

SPENDING

What Happened Where?

Great Plains About 2.5 million people left the plains during the severe drought of the 1930s.

California

N
W E
S

| 0 | 150 | 300 mi |
| 0 | 150 | 300 km |

GREAT PLAINS

California Hundreds of thousands of people fleeing the Dust Bowl moved to California. Many became migrant farmworkers.

New York City Six thousand jobless men sold apples on the streets of New York City during the early days of the Depression.

Chicago

New York City

Chicago, Illinois At the 1932 Democratic National Convention, Franklin Roosevelt first used the phrase "new deal." It later became the collective name of his economic programs to deal with the Great Depression.

Dust Bowl area

Other areas damaged by dust storms

The End of the Depression

World War II created a new demand for factory workers in the United States.

The New Deal helped millions of Americans who were suffering during the Great Depression, but it did not end the Depression. It took a massive world war to make the U.S. economy healthy again.

World War II began in Europe in 1939. At that time, the unemployment rate in the United States was 17 percent.

BY THE END OF WORLD WAR II, WOMEN

The United States began gearing up for war, producing planes, ships, and other goods for its allies in Europe. By the time the country entered the war in 1941, the national unemployment rate had dropped below 10 percent for the first time in 10 years.

Over the next few years, millions of Americans went off to war. Others worked in the factories that helped power the war effort. The economy grew strong once again.

The years of hardship had changed Americans. Those who lived through the time of hunger and desperation never forgot it. Many Americans became more careful with their money. They were haunted by what had happened and fearful of what could happen again. Decades later, one man explained, "Survivors [of the Depression] are still ridin' with the ghost—the ghost of those days when things came hard."

Millions of soldiers fought abroad during World War II.

MADE UP A THIRD OF THE U.S. WORKFORC

INFLUENTIAL INDIVIDUALS

Herbert Hoover

Herbert Hoover (1874–1964) was the 31st president of the United States. He was president when the Great Depression began. He did not believe that the government should interfere with business or give aid directly to individuals. Many people blamed him for not doing more to help those in need during the Depression.

Franklin D. Roosevelt

Franklin D. Roosevelt (1882–1945) was the 32nd president of the United States. He led the nation throughout much of the Great Depression. He began a series of programs called the New Deal to help those in need, put people back to work, and stabilize the banking industry. Among the programs created under the New Deal was the Social Security system.

H. L. Hunt (1889–1974) worked in the oil industry and became one of the world's richest men. During the Great Depression, before he became rich, he spent time riding the rails.

Dorothea Lange (1895–1965) was a photographer remembered for her images of people in need during the Great Depression. Her work brought the faces and reality of people who were suffering to those who were not so unfortunate.

Berenice Abbott (1898–1991) was a photographer who worked for the Works Progress Administration in the 1930s. She was known for her photographs detailing life in New York City.

Woody Guthrie (1912–1967) was an influential folksinger and songwriter. He left his home state of Oklahoma during the time of the Dust Bowl and began riding the rails. Many of his songs express the concerns of people uprooted by the Great Depression. His most famous songs include "This Land Is Your Land" and "So Long, It's Been Good to Know Yuh."

Woody Guthrie

TIMELINE

1929

The stock market crashes on October 29, marking the beginning of the Great Depression.

1931

Drought hits the Great Plains.

1935

The Works Progress Administration is started; the Social Security Act becomes law.

1936

Dorothea Lange photographs migrant workers in California.

1932

Franklin D. Roosevelt is elected president.

1933

Franklin Roosevelt gives his first fireside chat; the unemployment rate reaches 25 percent; the Civilian Conservation Corps is founded.

1934

The Securities and Exchange Commission is established.

1940

The first monthly Social Security check is issued.

1941

The United States enters World War II; the U.S. unemployment rate falls below 10 percent.

LIVING HISTORY

Primary sources provide firsthand evidence about a topic. Witnesses to a historical event create primary sources. They include autobiographies, newspaper reports of the time, oral histories, photographs, and memoirs. A secondary source analyzes primary sources, and is one step or more removed from the event. Secondary sources include textbooks, encyclopedias, and commentaries. To view the following primary and secondary sources, go to www.factsfornow.scholastic.com. Enter in the keywords **Great Depression** and look for the Living History logo Σ¡.

Σ¡ **"Brother, Can You Spare a Dime?"** The song "Brother, Can You Spare a Dime?" became an anthem of the Great Depression. It was famously recorded by Bing Crosby, one of the most popular singers of the 20th century.

Σ¡ **Dorothea Lange's Photos** Photographer Dorothea Lange captured some of the most dramatic images of the Great Depression by traveling throughout California to document the lives of migrant workers.

Σ¡ **Fireside Chats** President Franklin D. Roosevelt's first fireside chat on March 12, 1933, aimed to calm the fears of the American people and outline the new president's plan for dealing with the nation's banking system.

Σ¡ **Ticker Tape** View ticker tape that shows the rapidly decreasing stock prices on Black Tuesday.

RESOURCES

Books

Bolden, Tonya. *FDR's Alphabet Soup: New Deal America, 1932–1939.* New York: Alfred A. Knopf, 2010.

Elish, Dan. *Franklin Delano Roosevelt.* Tarrytown, NY: Marshall Cavendish Benchmark, 2009.

Fitzgerald, Stephanie. *The New Deal: Rebuilding America.* Minneapolis: Compass Point Books, 2007.

Grant, R. G. *Why Did the Great Depression Happen?* New York: Gareth Stevens, 2011.

Sandler, Martin W. *The Dust Bowl Through the Lens: How Photography Revealed and Helped Remedy a National Disaster.* New York: Walker & Co., 2009.

Visit this Scholastic Web site for more information on the Great Depression:
www.factsfornow.scholastic.com
Enter the keywords Great Depression

GLOSSARY

bankrupt (BANK-ruhpt) not able to pay one's debts

civilian (suh-VIL-yuhn) having to do with people not in the military or the police

credit (KRED-it) the providing of money or goods with the understanding that they will be paid for later

deposits (di-PAH-zits) money put into bank accounts

depression (di-PRESH-uhn) a time when the economy of a country is shrinking and many people lose their jobs

drought (DROUT) a long period without rain

economists (i-KAHN-uh-mists) experts in the way the economy works

economy (i-KAHN-uh-mee) the system of buying, selling, making things, and managing money in a place

export (EK-sport) sending products to another country to sell them there

humanitarian (hyoo-man-ih-TAIR-ee-un) a person who works to help other people and improve their lives

installment (in-STAWL-muhnt) one of a series of regular payments over a period of time for a purchased object

migrant (MYE-gruhnt) a person who moves from one area to another

mortgage (MOHR-gij) a loan from a bank used to buy a house or other property

speculation (spek-yuh-LAY-shuhn) taking part in risky investments

stock (STAHK) a share of a company purchased as an investment

stockbrokers (STAHK-broh-kurz) people who buy and sell stocks and shares in companies on behalf of other people

INDEX

Page numbers in *italics* indicate illustrations.

ABOUT THE AUTHOR

Melissa McDaniel is a writer and editor originally from Portland, Oregon. She has a bachelor's degree in history and a master's degree in library science. McDaniel has written books for young people on subjects ranging from Ellis Island to the Powhatan Indians to life on the deep-sea floor. She lives in New York City with her husband, daughter, dog, and frog.